Ten Poems
about Sons

Candlestick Press

Published by:
Candlestick Press,
Diversity House, 72 Nottingham Road, Arnold, Nottingham NG5 6LF
www.candlestickpress.co.uk

Design and typesetting by Craig Twigg

Printed by Bayliss Printing Company Ltd of Worksop, UK

Selection © Jonathan Edwards, 2024

Cover illustration © Caroline Barker, 2024
https://www.carolinebarkerart.co.uk/

Candlestick Press monogram © Barbara Shaw, 2008

© Candlestick Press, 2024

ISBN 978 1 913627 07 2

Acknowledgements

The poems in this pamphlet are reprinted from the following books, all by permission of the publishers listed unless stated otherwise. Every effort has been made to trace the copyright holders of the poems published in this book. The editor and publisher apologise if any material has been included without permission, or without the appropriate acknowledgement, and would be glad to be told of anyone who has not been consulted.

Thanks are due to all the copyright holders cited below for their kind permission.

Emily Blewitt, *Poetry Wales 55.2*, by permission of the author and publisher. Josephine Corcoran, *Love and Stones* (Live Canon, 2023) by permission of the author and publisher. Glyn Edwards, *Vertebrae* (The Lonely Press, 2019) by permission of the author. Langston Hughes, *The Collected Poems of Langston Hughes* (Alfred A Knopf Inc., 1995) reproduced by permission of David Higham Associates. Jackie Kay, *Darling: New & Selected Poems* (Bloodaxe Books, 2007) www.bloodaxebooks.com. Galway Kinnell, *Selected Poems* (Bloodaxe Books, 2001) www.bloodaxebooks.com. Li-Young Lee, *From Blossoms: Selected Poems* (Bloodaxe Books, 2007) www.bloodaxebooks.com. David Morley, *Scientific Papers* (Carcanet Press, 2002). Sinéad Morrissey, *Parallax* (Carcanet Press, 2013). Naomi Shihab Nye, *Red Suitcase* (BOA Editions, 1994). Copyright © 1994 by Naomi Shihab Nye. Reprinted with the permission of The Permissions Company, LLC on behalf of BOA Editions, Ltd., www.boaeditions.org.

All permissions cleared courtesy of Dr Suzanne Fairless-Aitken – Swift Permissions swiftpermissions@gmail.com.

Where poets are no longer living, their dates are given.

Contents

How far along are you?

This week my baby is a raspberry.
I roll him around
my tongue, tease out
each eye-lashed segment.
Careful not to crush him.

The baby is now a navel orange.
I press my lips to his nib,
leave the faintest toothmarks.
Savour the fragrance
of bruised citrus, the oiled imprint
of skin on skin.

When my baby becomes
a banana, still a little green,
I turn him on his side and gently squeeze
apart the seam. Hear the squeak,
glimpse immaculate flesh inside.

He's the world in a cantaloupe.
Tough, veined on the outside.
Too big for my mouth.

We finish a watermelon.
He enters rooms
before I do, spits out cries
like little black pips.
I clutch him

like a netball
rotate my wrists
push out my chest
and throw
       him laughing
             to the crowd.

Emily Blewitt

from Posterity

ii Buying satsumas for my son

I look down and I see my son.
I am buying satsumas for him.
He feels my fingers close against his own.
He holds one arm up, half-surrendering.
He feels my fingers close against his own.
The clench and tang: the citrus-tongue unwinding.
He holds one arm up, half-surrendering
something he wants, but what, he can't yet say.
The clench and tang – that citrus-tongue unwinding
in his palm now, like the unwinding of a gift:
something he wants, but what he can't yet say
and he is barely breathing, holding it all
in his palm now. Like the unwinding of a gift
he uncurls his hand from mine
and he is barely breathing, holding it all.

David Morley

Shoulders

A man crosses the street in rain,
stepping gently, looking two times north and south:
because his son is asleep on his shoulder.

No car must splash him.
No car drive too near to his shadow.

This man carries the world's most sensitive cargo
but he's not marked.
Nowhere does his jacket say FRAGILE,
HANDLE WITH CARE.

His ear fills up with breathing.
He hears the hum of a boy's dream
deep inside him.

We're not going to be able
to live in this world
if we're not willing to do what he's doing
with one another.

The road will only be wide.
The rain will never stop falling.

Naomi Shihab Nye

Lighthouse

My son's awake at ten, stretched out along
his bunk beneath the ceiling, wired and watchful.
The end of August. Already the high-flung
daylight sky of our Northern solstice dulls
earlier and earlier to a clouded bowl;
his Star of David lamp and plastic moon
have turned the dusk to dark outside his room.

Across the Lough, where ferries venture blithely
and once a cruise ship, massive as a palace,
inched its brilliant decks to open sea –
a lighthouse starts its own nightlong address
in fractured signalling; it blinks and bats
the swingball of its beam, then stands to catch,
then hurls it out again beyond its parallax.

He counts each creamy loop inside his head,
each well-black interval, and thinks it just for him –
this gesture from a world that can't be entered:
the two of them partly curtained, partly seen,
upheld in a sort of boy-talk conversation
no one else can hear. That private place, it answers,
with birds and slatted windows – I've been there.

Sinéad Morrissey

Mother to Son

Well, son, I'll tell you:
Life for me ain't been no crystal stair.
It's had tacks in it,
And splinters,
And boards torn up,
And places with no carpet on the floor –
Bare.
But all the time
I'se been a-climbin' on,
And reachin' landin's,
And turnin' corners,
And sometimes goin' in the dark
Where there ain't been no light.
So boy, don't you turn back.
Don't you set down on the steps
'Cause you finds it's kinder hard.
Don't you fall now –
For I'se still goin', honey,
I'se still climbin',
And life for me ain't been no crystal stair.

Langston Hughes (1901 – 1967)

What to do with his old clothes?

You carefully roll each babygrow from the dusty suitcase,
hold it in outstretched arms, weigh the memory of him inside it,
and fold it as gently as a paper bird. I unwind every sculpture again
so I too can inhale the months it wore him. Such quiet spaces,
smoky with his first dreams, warm from his growing world.

We carve out excuses that delay, then prolong the day,
He was wearing that on his first Christmas morning...
we could use those buttons from his cardigan, patchwork his pants.
I stack clothes into columns and we are made mute by the acute
understanding of what this operation means. We fold back the tears,

topple turrets into black bags, hold each other. There is a draft somewhere
and the room seems as poorly lit as it did when you were pregnant
and we painted the unfurnished house in wintery evenings after work.
I am as empty as the luggage at the foot of the loft ladder,
holding you, as barren as our busy lives will now become.

Downstairs, our boy is asleep, his body a Babel tower,
his loud breaths prising the baby gate ajar, his tiny flesh
growing up and against and through his pyjamas, his uniform,
his leather jacket, his woollen suit, his funeral coat. Tomorrow,
I will put five bags in the car boot, one back in the attic.

Glyn Edwards

A Story

Sad is the man who is asked for a story
and can't come up with one.

His five-year-old son waits in his lap.
Not the same story, Baba. A new one.
The man rubs his chin, scratches his ear.

In a room full of books in a world
of stories, he can recall
not one, and soon, he thinks, the boy
will give up on his father.

Already the man lives far ahead, he sees
the day this boy will go. *Don't go!*
Hear the alligator story! The angel story once more!
You love the spider story. You laugh at the spider.
Let me tell it!

But the boy is packing his shirts,
he is looking for his keys. *Are you a god,*
the man screams, *that I sit mute before you?*
Am I a god that I should never disappoint?

But the boy is here. *Please, Baba, a story?*
It is an emotional rather than logical equation,
an earthly rather than heavenly one,
which posits that a boy's supplications
and a father's love add up to silence.

Li-Young Lee

Then, said I, Lord, How Long?

Beautiful, the man in my hallway
lacing up his second-hand shoes.
He is 18 years old, he is my son,
he is late, I have no money for him,
all my loose change
dropped in the church basket. *Holy Hell!*
They are using it to fly criminals around the world!

Waving goodbye is the man, shaved head
and beard, a time-lapse the hallway,
scuffed mornings. Boys and girls calling
to walk him to school, billowing
like fruits and flowers, disappearing –
reappearing like film stars to crowd
the hallway mirror, perfume the house.

Tripping over, stepping around
rucksacks, hats, gadgets, mud,
musical instruments, books,
sleeping bags, corner shop alcohol –
Did you hand in your essay?
Mum, the planet is dying –
Goodbye, goodbye, for 18 years, waving goodbye.

Hungry the baby, sucking his fists,
cold hospital February, scored plastic cot,
my nipples already scabbing
and him three hours old,
as they stitched me, he latched on to my breast,
cuts on his face, bruises, mini prize fighter,
starched blanket, milk, the heat of him.

Next to the candles I sat, next to the Virgin Mary,
reading Isiah backwards
in my head, holding language
in my mouth to taste it longer.
desolate utterly be land the & man without houses the &
inhabitant without wasted be cities the until answered he
& long how Lord I said.

Then.
Give me a kiss then, Mum. I'm away.
Eighteen summers
shaken from trees, falling flowers, leaves
raining down, streaming,
through park, town, along the street,
into my hallway, my childless house.

Josephine Corcoran

Gap Year

(for Mateo)

I

I remember your Moses basket before you were born.
I'd stare at the fleecy white sheet for days, weeks,
willing you to arrive, hardly able to believe
I would ever have a real baby to put in the basket.

I'd feel the mound of my tight tub of a stomach,
and you moving there, foot against my heart,
elbow in my ribcage, turning, burping, awake, asleep.
One time I imagined I felt you laugh.

I'd play you Handel's *Water Music* or Emma Kirkby
singing Pergolesi. I'd talk to you, my close stranger,
call you Tumshie, ask when you were coming to meet me.
You arrived late, the very hot summer of eighty-eight.

You had passed the due date string of eights,
and were pulled out with forceps, blue, floury,
on the fourteenth of August on Sunday afternoon.
I took you home on Monday and lay you in your basket.

II

Now, I peek in your room and stare at your bed
hardly able to imagine you back in there sleeping,
your handsome face – soft, open. Now you are eighteen,
six foot two, away, away in Costa Rica, Peru, Bolivia.

I follow your trails on my *Times Atlas*:
from the Caribbean side of Costa Rica to the Pacific,
the baby turtles to the massive leatherbacks.
Then on to Lima, to Cuzco. Your grandfather

rings: 'Have you considered altitude sickness,
Christ, he's sixteen thousand feet above sea level.'
Then to the lost city of the Incas, Macchu Picchu,
where you take a photograph of yourself with the statue

of the original Tupac. You are wearing a Peruvian hat.
Yesterday in Puno before catching the bus for Copacabana,
you suddenly appear on a webcam and blow me a kiss,
you have a new haircut; your face is grainy, blurry.

Seeing you, shy, smiling, on the webcam reminds me
of the second scan at twenty weeks, how at that fuzzy
moment back then, you were lying cross-legged with
an index finger resting sophisticatedly on one cheek.

You started the Inca trail in Arctic conditions
and ended up in subtropical. Now you plan the Amazon
in Bolivia. Your grandfather rings again to say
'There's three warring factions in Bolivia, warn him

against it. He canny see everything. Tell him to come home.'
But you say all the travellers you meet rave about Bolivia. You want
to see the Salar de Uyuni,
the world's largest salt-flats, the Amazonian rainforest.

And now you are not coming home till four weeks after
your due date. After Bolivia, you plan to stay
with a friend's Auntie in Argentina.
Then – to Chile where you'll stay with friends of Diane's.

And maybe work for the Victor Jara Foundation.
I feel like a home-alone mother; all the lights
have gone out in the hall, and now I am
wearing your large black slippers, flip-flopping

into your empty bedroom, trying to imagine you
in your bed. I stare at the photos you send by messenger:
you on the top of the world, arms outstretched, eager.
Blue sky, white snow; you by Lake Tararhua, beaming.

My heart soars like the birds in your bright blue skies.
My love glows like the sunrise over the lost city.
I sing along to Ella Fitzgerald, *A tisket A tasket*.
I have a son out in the big wide world.

A flip and a skip ago, you were dreaming in your basket.

Jackie Kay

After Making Love We Hear Footsteps

For I can snore like a bullhorn
or play loud music
or sit up talking with any reasonably sober Irishman
and Fergus will only sink deeper
into his dreamless sleep, which goes by all in one flash,
but let there be that heavy breathing
or a stifled come-cry anywhere in the house
and he will wrench himself awake
and make for it on the run – as now, we lie together,
after making love, quiet, touching along the length of our bodies,
familiar touch of the long-married,
and he appears – in his baseball pajamas, it happens,
the neck opening so small he has to screw them on –
and flops down between us and hugs us and snuggles himself to sleep,
his face gleaming with satisfaction at being this very child.

In the half darkness we look at each other
and smile
and touch arms across this little, startlingly muscled body –
this one whom habit of memory propels to the ground of his making,
sleeper only the mortal sounds can sing awake,
this blessing love gives again into our arms.

Galway Kinnell (1927 – 2014)